UNACCOMPANIED

Ta'Sean McKinley

Copyright © 2015 by Ta'Sean McKinley

All rights reserved. No part of this book may be produced, stored in a retrieval system, or transmitted in any form, or by any means, electronic, mechanical, photocopying, recording or otherwise, without prior permission of the author.

ISBN: 978-0-9912913-1-1

Edited by Tyler Kelly

Cover image by Carlis Howze

Cover design by Christopher Roberts of IAMIMAGE.com

Interior design and formatting by Karolyne Roberts of IAMIMAGE.com

Unless otherwise indicated, scripture quotations are from The Holy Bible, New Living Translation © 1996, 2004, 2007 by Tyndale House Foundation. All rights reserved.

King James Version (KJV) © 1989 Thomas Nelson, Inc. All rights reserved.

For pricing on bulk orders email taseanmckinley@gmail.com

TABLE OF CONTENTS

DEDICATION 6

FOREWORD 7

CHAPTER 1: "ABANDONED" 10

CHAPTER 2: "SOMETHING MISSING" 20

CHAPTER 3: "TRUE LOVE" 27

CHAPTER 4: "THE STRUGGLE OF FORGIVENESS" 34

CHAPTER 5: "A UN-REPENTED HEART" 43

CHAPTER 6: "THE FIGHT TO OVERCOME" 50

CHAPTER 7: "THE TESTING OF FAITH" 58

CHAPTER 8: "TAKING THE FIRST STEP" 70

CHAPTER 9: "LACKING PRAYER" 79

CHAPTER 10: "WHAT DID I SIGN UP FOR?" 90

TA'SEAN MCKINLEY

DEDICATION

This book is dedicated to my lovely wife Stepphina Renee McKinley. You have cheered me on though out this whole process and you've always believed in me no matter how crazy my ideas sound. Also, to my daughter (Baby McKinley.) I love you both with all of my heart. You both mean the world to me. I will forever love, protect, serve and lead you both as I receive instructions from The Lord; for the rest of my life. I pray that the words that are contained in this book will be a guide for you both even after I pass away.

FOREWORD

This is a soul-stirring book you have in your hands. There are many men who say many things, but there are only a few men who say things that are worth saying. Ta'Sean is one of those few men.

Ta'Sean touches on some very sensitive and personal areas of his life. It is a step forward in confronting past offenses and unforgettable life circumstances. He uses his personal stories to encourage the reader to dive deep into their heart and past and overcome through and by the power of Jesus Christ.

Fully embrace what you are about to read. Take time to reflect on your own difficulties and allow the words to captivate your heart. This book is not like the others. Ta'Sean uses firsthand experiences to captivate, encourage, inspire and convict. You will not be disappointed.

I thank God for the opportunity to know this man who walks with God. He and his wife are true treasures to the Body of Christ. I celebrate him and the work he has done in this book.

Be encouraged and inspired by what you read. The words written therein will challenge the readers to live

Foreword

courageously, serve the Lord wholeheartedly and give of themselves generously.

God bless.

-Cornelius Lindsey

Senior Pastor of The Gathering Oasis Church,

Atlanta, Georgia

Husband. Author. Friend.

www.corneliuslindsey.com

Chapter 1: Abandoned

Chapter 1: Abandoned

> "And about the ninth hour Jesus cried with a loud voice, saying, Eli, Eli, lama sabachthani? that is to say, My God, my God, why hast thou forsaken me?"
>
> (Matthew 27:46 KJV)

Ta'Sean McKinley

Have you ever been at a place in life where you felt like God abandoned you? Like He set you on a path to a destination, you followed the path with obedience, but then suddenly He seemed to have disappeared? He got totally quiet on you. Ever felt abandoned by the person that you were most close to? Like you really needed them and all of a-sudden they were no longer there for you? It is a hurtful feeling to be abandoned physically, I would agree; but what about when people are physically present but spiritually absent? Physically you see them and they are smiling, laughing, and having a good time with you, but deep on the inside they are hurting and you are hurting to. Yet, neither one of you has ever had the guts to open up and confess your issues and daily struggles with one

Chapter 1: Abandoned

another. The truth is you both are too afraid of letting your guard down for fear of seeming weak. The sad thing is that we often focus on those who have abandoned us and we neglect to direct our focus on who we have abandoned.

Growing up I always felt as though I was alone. I always felt like no one understood me or the situations that I was dealing with on the inside I felt like my struggles and thoughts were exclusive to me. I believed that no one battled with these same issues. It seemed like even though I was in a room full of people, I was still alone. I felt like I was right in the middle of family and loved ones with a heart full of secrets, questions, and thoughts ready to spill out, but I was afraid that I would be looked at differently, so I kept them imprisoned within. After all, these were some really messed up feelings and embarrassing thoughts. I constantly wondered how others would view me if I shared with them what was really going on with me. Would they still like me? Would they think I was weak? What if they called me crazy for "thinking too deep" into things? As these thoughts and worries continued to play in my head, I began to hold in all of my thoughts, secrets, questions, and feelings because I was afraid that people would say negative things about me and worried about how they would treat me.

It was not until I met my wife that I began to share some of my secrets and really open up to someone else. Because we both opened up to one another I was able to realize that I wasn't alone. It was at that moment when I

Chapter 1: Abandoned

recognized that no one's life is as perfect as it may seem and that I'm not alone in the issues that I face on a daily basis I wasn't the only person that dealt with problems of rejection, living with a false identity, feeling lonely, feeling misunderstood, feeling unwanted by peers, etc. We began to confide in each other and it really helped us both to express ourselves in a way that I once saw impossible. I thought people would never be able to do this because of the fear of feeling vulnerable and uncomfortable. It was a relief to know that I wasn't the only person that felt the way I felt or battled the fights that I battle. I was not alone, there was finally someone that could relate to me and see life out of the same lens as myself. It was a relief to know that I could be open and share things that I held in my heart for the longest. It was a huge burden that was lifted off of me. I no longer had to walk around with those burdens weighing me down. The feeling was priceless.

One day I took some time to myself and thought if my wife and I held in many of the same struggles and feelings in our hearts for this long; how many other people in the world do the same. How many other people continue to deal with issues of the heart simply because so many people are afraid to share their current and past struggles? Most people do not feel comfortable opening up to others because they feel like they are the only ones dealing with their situation and no one else can relate. It seems like everyone else is living or has lived a perfect life. In reality everyone has a testimony. Everyone has a story that they

Chapter 1: Abandoned

can share to help someone else. The problem is that no one wants to speak up because of the fear of being looked upon differently.

There are things that we are going to go through throughout this book that you may experience at different levels as you continue to walk with Christ. Many people struggle in areas such as feeling abandoned, feeling empty, looking for love in all the wrong places, holding grudges that should have been let go of a long time ago, etc. This book will help give a little insight along with personal experience on how to deal with different situations and how to overcome different seasons in your life. I want to share with you some things that I've personally experienced over time that I have struggled with. I want to share them with you to encourage you along the journey. I want to assure you that you are not the only person that is struggling with the conditions of your heart. There are many people who are dealing or have dealt with similar situations and I am one of them. As a follower of Christ we have to be willing to give up our pride and share what God has brought us through so that He can get the glory and so that lives can be transformed.

You are not in this race alone. I've felt like I was alone for the longest and I had the misperception that everyone around me never was tempted with the things that I was tempted with or faced with the things that I've faced. I want you to know that real people have real problems and God has a real solution.

Chapter 1: Abandoned

Consider the questions below before reading:

1. Have you given your Heart to Jesus?

2. Does everything you do reflect Jesus?

3. What are some of the secrets you have kept in for a long time because you were afraid of what people would say?

4. What are you struggling with at the moment?

5. Are you willing to yield and allow God to change you?

: "Something Missing"

Chapter 2: "Something Missing"

"But God commendeth his love toward us, in that, while we were yet sinners, Christ died for us. Much more then, being now justified by his blood, we shall be saved from wrath through him."

(Romans 5:8-9 KJV)

Ta'Sean McKinley

Have you ever felt like something was missing in your life? That feeling you get like you know you are forgetting something or missing something that you are suppose to have? For example, Often times I lose my train of thought if I am interrupted or distracted by something. I know that what I was about to say was important, and I feel like I'm going to go crazy if I don't remember what it was or say what I intended to say. This could possibly be the case with you.

Spiritually you know that you are missing something; but you often get interrupted and distracted when you know that your spirit is longing to be fed. Every time you grab your bible to read that evil and rude spirit of sleepiness comes upon you. Now you can't get past three

Chapter 2: "Something Missing"

verses before you find yourself asleep at 3 o'clock in the afternoon. Every time you begin to get into a position of prayer and true focus, your phone rings or you realize that you left the T.V on and you hear something that strikes your attention so you begin to give the T.V the time that you set out to give God.

Then you find yourself empty for the remainder of the day because you thought that you did something that you never really did. Now you feel as though you are missing something but you just can't place your finger on it. It seems harder to read the word in the time we live in today, because of all of the distractions (e.g., phones, video games, television, social media) we have access to. These things make us feel like we are being productive, but in reality we really are just wasting a bunch of time. Social media is one of the biggest distractions I've had to deal with. Reading up on the latest things that people are doing, saying, and posting seems more compelling and interesting than reading the word at times. But, we have to come to a point where we are so desperate to know the heart of God that we will do whatever it take to get that much closer to him, to know him just that much more. The problem with some of us is that we'd rather be on social media then get closer to the creature of the universe. We'd rather read their back and forth comments then to read and compare the Old Testament from the New Testament.

Chapter 2: "Something Missing"

I must admit, at times it gets challenging to read the word and spend that alone time with Jesus, it does. Yet, we have to have such a desire on the inside of us that we just can't live without that alone time with him. We have come to the conclusion that everything outside of Jesus will fail. Only what we do for him will last and it should be our hearts desire to spend our entire existence with our Savior.

God desires our time. Jesus wants that intimate time with you, so He can talk to you, love on you, and teach you. This is why we can't be distracted and interrupted with the things of the world and our everyday life. Jesus literally died for you so that he can spend the rest of eternity with you. He literally died so that you can be with him forever. God didn't want to be without you that's how much he loves you. While we were deep in our sins Christ still cared for us and loved us so much that he gave us his all. He gave us everything that he had to offer. Let's get to that place where we return the favor and realize that we can't live without Christ and be willing to give up everything just to spend eternity with Him!

Chapter 3: "True Love"

Ta'Sean McKinley

"This is how much God loved the world: He gave his Son, his one and only Son. And this is why: so that no one need be destroyed; by believing in him, anyone can have a whole and lasting life. God didn't go to all the trouble of sending his Son merely to point an accusing finger, telling the world how bad it was. He came to help, to put the world right again. Anyone who trusts in him is acquitted; anyone who refuses to trust him has long since been under the death sentence without knowing it. And why? Because of that person's failure to believe in the one-of-a-kind Son of God when introduced to him."

(John 3:16-18 MSG)

Chapter 3: "True Love"

I have always been the type to want a love that would never change up on me. I started searching for that love in people and I soon discovered they would fail me every time. Most males would never admit that they too want to be loved, because being vulnerable in this way portrays weakness or being soft, both of which titles men work to avoid. The truth is, everyone, male or female wants to be loved, it is a part of our human nature; sometimes we all just show it in different ways. However, it seemed to me as if no one would ever love me the way I desired in my heart to be loved. So after many disappointments and much hurt, my heart turned cold towards people and I never let anyone get close to me. I felt as though no one would ever be what I needed them to be. (Which was crazy because in all actuality I was looking for them to take the place of God and love me how only he could love me.) I was walking around trying to hold people to a standard that they will never be able to amount to. Because of my own ignorance, I held grudges towards others and my heart was filled with unforgiveness.

Thank God I came to know Jesus! A guy that to me was always a joke. After all, the preacher is up here screaming to the top of his lungs, talking about "He had 2 fish and fed 5,000 men." I always thought to myself, "I know I'm young but, I can still do math bruh". Not to mention the woman that sat behind me was always jumping up and down hitting me all in my arm and I had to sit there looking straight ahead trying to keep a straight face and act like

Chapter 3: "True Love"

she didn't hurt my arm. Then to top it all off, these people kept saying that she "caught the Holy Ghost." I'm like, "Wait. Now I'm scared." "Did a ghost just come in here and jump into this lady and I didn't even see it?" Even though this is a little humorous these were my actual thoughts. I was extremely lost.

Then one day I began to feel a love that I had never felt before. A love that I was missing and that I had always longed for. God began to show himself more clearly to me day by day. Just to know that no matter what I have done in the past, no matter what I will do, he would always love me even though he knows exactly what every one of my flaws are. I believe the song writer said "you see the depths of my heart and you love me the same." His love is simply amazing. The feeling of His love was so amazing, I was completely over whelmed. I'm amazed at God's never ending, never failing, never changing love. It puts me in a place of comfort. I've learned that God gives us another chance every day we wake up to overcome the battle we lost in the days before.

1 Corinthians 13:4-7 (NIV) says "Love is patient, love is kind. It does not envy, it does not boast, it is not proud. It does not dishonor others, it is not self-seeking, it is not easily angered, it keeps no record of wrongs. Love does not delight in evil but rejoices with the truth. It always protects, always trusts, always hopes, always perseveres." This is not only a breakdown of how your love towards others should be but how God's love towards us is also.

Chapter 3: "True Love"

Many of us often Believe that after we mess up God somehow doesn't love us anymore. We believe after we made a bad mistake God will neglect us. The fact of the matter is that God will never leave you nor forsake you. If you have made a mistake and have repented in your heart God is faithful to forgive you. We have to repent and turn our backs towards sin and all unrighteousness. God's love is perfect and unconditional. His love is available to you today, it was yesterday, and will be tomorrow. I challenge you to except it!

Chapter 4: "The Struggle of Forgiveness"

Chapter 4: "The Struggle of Forgiveness"

> "For if you forgive other people when they sin against you, your heavenly Father will also forgive you. But if you do not forgive others their sins, your Father will not forgive your sins."
>
> (Matthew 6:14-15 NIV)

Ta'Sean McKinley

Sometimes one of the most challenging things for us to do as humans is to forgive. It's challenging to forgive that person that walked out of your life when you thought you needed them the most. It's tough to forgive that person that told a lie about you to your peers. It's tough to forgive that person that smiles in your face, but you know that behind their smile they can't wait to see you fail. It's hard to forgive that person that told you they loved you and that they would never leave you, but they only used you, mistreated you, degraded you, and then left you. It's a challenge to forgive that mother or that father who wasn't in your life to be there for you and guide and direct you as a parent should. I understand how it feels to hold bitterness in your heart toward people that have

Chapter 4: "The Struggle of Forgiveness"

mistreated you. I know how it feels to let pain linger in your heart for days, and those days turn into weeks, and those weeks turn into months, and those months turn into years, and eventually you never get past the pain. You never talk about the pain to anyone, because you feel as if no one understands. It hurts you on the inside just to think about talking about the pain of your past. Besides, even if they did understand you feel as though you should be a tougher person. Then you rationalize within yourself that you are just complaining and your feelings sound stupid or common.

Ultimately, you may realize that you never forgave that person that mistreated you or offended you, and you find yourself with this bitter heart of unforgiveness. I want to let you know that today is the day that you can begin to be set free from that hurt, free from that pain, free from the abuse, neglect, and misuse. You no longer have to walk around with bitterness carrying around with you things from that persons past. Allowing them to live for free in your mind. (If you are ready to be free stop reading this book and begin to pray to the father. I'm not telling you what to pray, but I am telling you when you pray the Lord hears your prayer, and in due time he will answer you if you go to him humble and with a pure heart.)

Forgiveness is not always the easiest thing to do. As a believer we have to practice having a spirit of forgiveness. We have to strive to forgive others how our father forgives us. We cannot afford to have contingencies on our

Chapter 4: "The Struggle of Forgiveness"

forgiveness. We have to make up in our minds that we will forgive others no matter the cost, no matter how much it hurts us, no matter how much forgiving them makes us feel like we are losing. Forgiveness must be the reaction of the believer against all hurt and disappointment. When someone offends you your reaction must in turn be forgiveness. Matthew 6:14-15 tells us that the way we react to others when they sin against us will be the same way our Heavenly Father will react towards us when we sin against him. It's that deep. It is a must for us to forgive because we will one day be in need of forgiveness. Depending upon how you forgave those who offended you, will be the access or denial of your forgiveness from the Father. Forgiveness has to take place in our hearts on a daily basis. It is mandatory.

Forgiveness is not an option for the believer. Many of us walk around as if we are entitled to have the option to forgive or not. As a believer forgiveness comes with the territory. Our savior requires us to forgive and that's exactly what we should do. Unforgiveness is birthed from a selfish mindset. It is a mindset that says it's all about me, my feelings, my heart aches, my trust that has been abused, the hurt they caused me, how they used me. It's all about me, me, me, me, me. It's all about how you feel and how they hurt and offended you. That's why we are instructed to constantly keep our eyes off of ourselves and others, and focus only on Christ. Once you focus on Christ

Chapter 4: "The Struggle of Forgiveness"

then you will have a better perspective and can see things from a different angle.

I can honestly say that I have had to work on my forgiveness muscle. It wasn't always easy but as I continued to forgive people for the small things when something that felt major came my way I was able to let go and forgive them more easily. We have to come to the understanding that people will always fail us. It could be your spouse, your child, your parents, a co-worker, your pastor, your best-friend. It doesn't matter who they are, if they have breath and they have flesh they are not exempt from the possibility of one day hurting you. Though it may not always be intentional, it will happen, and it will still require you to forgive them. God requires us to forgive our brothers and sisters and those who mistreat us. He demands that we forgive others as Christ has forgiven us. So as believers we have to exercise our forgiveness muscle, so that when the time comes, our spirit will rise over our flesh and we will be able to forgive anyone for anything that we ourselves wouldn't be able to forgive.

Chapter 5: "A Un-repented Heart"

"If we confess our sins, he is faithful and just to forgive us our sins, and to cleanse us from all unrighteousness. If we say that we have not sinned, we make him a liar, and his word is not in us."

(1 John 1:9-10 KJV)

Chapter 5: "A Un-repented Heart"

What does it mean to have a repented heart? How do I repent? The Greek word for repent is Metaneó which means to change one's mind. I repent, change my mind, change the inner man (particularly with reference to acceptance of the will of God). If you struggle with admitting that you're wrong or admitting that the way you say, do, or think isn't always right then you really need to examine yourself and be willing to yield your heart to God and allow The Holy Spirit to convict you.

There was a time in my life where I did, said, and reacted however I wanted to. In reality, I was very self-centered. Everything had to revolve around me, and I didn't care how my reactions affected anyone around me. I definitely didn't care about how my reactions pleased or displeased God. He was absolutely the last thing on my mind. I could have really cared less about how my actions made him feel. I just wanted to "be me" and do as I pleased.

As my relationship with Jesus grows, and as your grows, we will begin to get more in line with the will of God for our lives and more in tune with The Holy Spirit. (This happens only through prayer.) The Holy Spirit will lead us and guide us into all truth. God's Holy Spirit will speak to you and tell you, "Hey, you know that's not right." "You know you need to go apologize." "I need you to get rid of that." "Go there, and say this." The Holy Spirit speaks to us often but we choose to ignore Him. We allow our flesh to take rule over The Spirit because we are not spending

Chapter 5: "A Un-repented Heart"

enough time disciplining our self in prayer and in The Word. We have become too busy feeding our flesh with the things of this world and our own lustful desires, opposed to feeding our spirit.

God desires you to give Him your all. God doesn't want half of you. He wants to have all of you to Himself. When we truly repent God will forgive us for all of our sins. God's forgiveness is never ending and it's never failing. God is right there with open arms waiting for you to repent (turn from your wickedness and have a change of heart) and come to Him. He is waiting for you to lay aside all of your sins and turn away from them and come running after Him. God's desire is to forgive you, embrace you, and love on you, but instead of running to Him you constantly insist on running from Him with an extra luggage of sin right along with you. God is so amazing. His ways are not our ways and his thoughts are not our thoughts. Open up your heart and allow the Holy Spirit to lead you into repentance.

It actually takes a strong person to humble their self and repent. If you are struggling with repenting, you may be on the weak side. Being able to admit when you are wrong and turning away from sin is a sign of strength. It is a sign that you know that you are not perfect or have it all together. You understand that only God is perfect and his commandment and His conviction is holy and just. The weak spirited person gives in to temptation and does whatever he or she wants to do. The person that is

Chapter 5: "A Un-repented Heart"

strengthened in the spirit says that even though I am presented with something that makes my flesh go crazy I have standards, I have morals, I have an obligation to my Father, to only do what is pleasing in his sight.

No, it isn't always the easiest or the simplest of tasks starting off, but as you continue to work that spiritual muscle of saying no and rejecting sin it will soon become second nature. We should repent daily and continue to ask God to cleanse us from the inside out. Will you choose to turn from all sin and unrighteousness?

Chapter 6: "The Fight to Overcome"

"And they overcame him by the blood of the Lamb, and by the word of their testimony; and they loved not their lives unto the death."

(Revelation 12:11 KJV)

Ta'Sean McKinley

"I feel stuck in this position. I want to quit what I'm doing but for some reason I can't get past this phase in my life. I know it's not right but this feeling just overtakes me and I can't get past it. I've tried but I simply just can't." I know how you feel. I hear you, and part of what you're feeling is right. You can't. But God can. With God all things are possible to them that believe.

The more you spend time with Jesus and the more you yield to the Holy Spirit, you will soon overcome that thing you once thought that you couldn't overcome. God will begin to take the desire to fulfill the lust of the flesh out of your heart. You will begin to strive to please God and the fear of the Lord will be your strength. When sin presents itself you will be so God conscious that you instantly think

Chapter 6: "The Fight to Overcome"

"will my actions please God." "Am I operating in integrity?" Sooner than you know, it will become easier to flee from and reject sin.

I use to struggle a lot with watching pornography. I felt as though I couldn't do without it. I felt as if I would never be able to overcome it. Pornography had a hold on me. I would literally watch porn any and everywhere. That's how much it had a grip on my life. I thought that this sin would be with me until I died. It was that deep. If I could be totally transparent, the temptation still comes up sometimes but the difference between now and then is that reverence that I have toward God so it doesn't phase me like it used to. I've realized that I can overcome my temptation by my faith in Jesus! I've realized that He is all that I need and the filth of porn will never be able to satisfy me.

There are many different temptations and obstacles to overcome. What is a challenge for one person may not necessarily be a challenge for the next. Nevertheless, we are all challenged and tempted in some area in our life. The question isn't whether or not we are challenged, but more so how we handle and conduct ourselves when we are challenged. It is important to constantly focus on doing what is pleasing in the sight of God and allowing the Holy Spirit to be your guide. This is the key to overcoming.

I shared my testimony to let you know that I understand how you feel. I have been in your shoes in one

Chapter 6: "The Fight to Overcome"

way or another. We are all trying to overcome something. I just wanted to encourage you and let you know that you can overcome. Their is a hope, and that hope is in Jesus. Jesus always gives us a way of escape; He always provides a way for us to overcome. We just have to choose to take the option that He provides for us constantly. Having an intimate relationship with Jesus will give you that strength and the power to overcome sin. The question is how bad do you want to overcome? Do you really want to please God? Do you really want to turn away from your sin(s)?

I dare you to open up your heart to Jesus. I dare you to spend time in His Word. I dare you to spend time with Jesus in prayer. Just spend that alone time with Him and allow Him to transform you. Allow Jesus to lead you on the path of righteousness. Be intentional in your alone time with God. Whatever you desire of God go to Him in prayer and He will not only hear you, but He will answer you.

When you overcome (and you will overcome) you will feel great! You will know that it was only by the hand of God that you were able to overcome. I have tried and tried to overcome pornography and it would last for a day or two but I would always run right back to it, like a dog running back to its vomit. It's not always an easy task, but as we work on that muscle of self-denial and resist self-gratification we get stronger at declining sins offer. One day we will be so used to saying no to sin that it doesn't even bother us anymore and it won't be a struggle at all.

Chapter 6: "The Fight to Overcome"

You are an overcomer. You can overcome, you will overcome, and you must overcome.

Chapter 7: "The Testing of Faith"

Chapter 7: "The Testing of Faith"

"Trust in him at all times, you people; pour out your hearts to him, for God is our refuge."

(Psalm 62:8 NIV)

Ta'Sean McKinley

Many of us have issues with trust. These days it's hard to trust in relationships. It's hard to trust our government. It's hard to trust our surroundings. It's hard to trust our bank accounts. It's even often at times hard to trust ourselves. Ultimately, our trust has been misused so much that it's hard to trust anyone or anything. Still, God demands for us to trust. In fact without your trust in God you can't even please Him. You have to have total faith in Him. I used the word trust because without your trust in God you will not be able to operate in faith.

Trust is simply to believe in the reliability, truth, ability, or strength of someone or something. So to say that you have faith in God, is to say you completely trust Him. When you totally place your faith in God you are not

Chapter 7: "The Testing of Faith"

depending on your own efforts, but you are standing on His word and relying only on Him. If He told you to do something and you obey what it is that He has told you to do, it is His job to put all of the pieces together not yours. Don't take it upon yourself to do what you think you should do or what sounds good to you. Don't move until He tells you to and if He doesn't say anything wait patiently and continue dwelling in His presence until He does. Ask yourself this question, are your relying fully on God or are you depending on your own efforts?

Faith causes us to go into a state of complete dependency. We have to be able to only depend on Jesus to carry out the plan that He has for us. Faith is not moving because you can see, faith is moving when you can't see.

Most of us were raised on this independent mindset that says, I don't need anyone, I can do it all by myself. I don't need anyone's guidance, help, and/or advice. Then we take this worldly mindset and we operate in this mindset when we are dealing with The Almighty.

Faith causes us to rely completely on God so we have this idea that when we are walking by faith we are taking a "chance." When considering following the instructions of God, we may often associate listening to God's voice as a risk. In the time we live in today we seem to have more faith in people then we do in God. We have become so dependent on the things we can see, that in turn, we have pushed having faith totally out of the equation. We only seem to operate in faith when we are down to our last or

Chapter 7: "The Testing of Faith"

have no other options. We treat God as a last resort option instead of The Author of our lives. It's only when the doctor says your family member has three weeks to live that now you want to trust God and use your "faith" for Him to do something in your life. Or when you find yourself in a tough position with no way out, you run to God and try to use Him as an escape from your situation. Faith is not asking God to do. Faith is listening to the voice of God and doing. We have to seek God's counsel and guidance at all times. We must continually go before God in prayer asking, what do you require of me? What is it that you want me to do? What is it that you want me to stop doing? Please don't wait until you find yourself in a bad position to decide to go to God for help. We should look to God for our next move on a daily basis.

So why do we look at having faith in God as taking a chance rather than a guarantee? God tells us to do something and we say "well that's too risky" or "I don't know how that's going to work." Well duh... that's what faith is, you're not supposed to know. When God tells you to do something it is always for your benefit. No matter what it looks like, it is always for your benefit. Well what if it hurts? It's for your benefit. What if it's uncomfortable? It's for your benefit. What if it means I lose everything I have? It's for your benefit. God will not tell you to do anything that he knows will not benefit you in the long run.

Chapter 7: "The Testing of Faith"

When we think of something benefiting us we think of something that is in our best interest and gives us some form of gain immediately. The concept is right but the timing is wrong. We have to learn to be patient and wait on The Lord. He will in due time reward us. We are supposed to store up our treasures in heaven, which means we don't have access to our treasures yet, but when we get there we will receive our reward from Jesus. The worldly mindset says "pay me now!" But as a follower of Christ we know that one day Jesus will reward us and it will be a public reward.

We as people seem to have more faith in humans then we do in God. If a human tells us something, we believe them almost instantly with little questioning. If God were to tell us something we almost instantly go into a state of questioning and reasoning. If your boss tells you to work for two weeks and they will send you a paycheck in the mail, we believe them with no questions asked. We wait patiently in expectation for the check to come. We don't constantly think to ourselves, maybe the check will come, maybe it won't, we have total faith that it is going to come at its expected time. Now if God tells us to do the same thing we would question it. How are you going to give me the check? Where is it going to come from? God, who do you bank with? Chase? We have so many questions and so much doubt instead of just believing God and patiently waiting in expectation. How much more will God stay true

Chapter 7: "The Testing of Faith"

to his word then your boss on your job? Who will you put your faith in? Men? Or The Creator?

Now faith is the substance of things hoped for, the evidence of things not seen (Hebrews 11:1 KJV). It is only by your faith that God can carry out the plan He has for your life. God requires your faith to be active. Your faith is the key to open the door to the next level that God has prepared for you. It says that "faith is the substance of things hoped for," substance, being a tangible matter or a tangible thing. It is that tangible faith that is the evidence of things not seen. Our faith is the evidence that the things that God has told us that we can't see is about to come to past. I encourage you today to seek God with your whole heart and ask Him what it is that He requires of you. Hear His voice clearly and obey Him no matter the cost.

I never knew what faith was until God told me to move to Atlanta. I had an idea of what I thought faith was but I never fully depended on God before. I always had to have some type of control over my situation in order to have what I considered, faith. There always had to be some type of solid evidence in order for me to do anything concerning faith. Then God had to show me that I was never depending totally on him, in fact I was depending on myself and my own efforts. The Lord told me to move and don't take anything with me or make any plans and that He was going to lead me. Of course it was a challenge but it was a challenge that I couldn't refuse. I had received

Chapter 7: "The Testing of Faith"

instructions from the infinite God to totally depend on Him and He was going to take care of me and my family. So that's what I did and He walked with me and led me the whole way. Will you totally neglect your will to follow the will of God?

Chapter 8: "Taking the First Step"

"But without faith it is impossible to please him: for he that cometh to God must believe that he is, and that he is a rewarder of them that diligently seek him."

(Hebrews 11:6 KJV)

Ta'Sean McKinley

How frightening is it to be told to believe in something that you can't see? The questions that we often have in our minds become endless. The thoughts become mind boggling. Things that we once were familiar with starts to even become questionable around us.

One of the most precious things we have as a child is our imagination. Our imagination can take us places human reasoning can't comprehend. Have you ever thought about where you would be in the future when you were younger? We've all heard the question, "what do you want to be when you grow up?" We all had different answers but in reality we never knew what we would become. Although while we were stating what we wanted to become, we began to see a picture of ourselves as who

Chapter 8: "Taking the First Step"

we stated we wanted to be. This allowed our statement concerning the future to become more believable. The problem with most of us is that the world has tainted our imagination and has convinced people to only think with reason. Have you ever let your imagination run wild while thinking about the Glory of God?

I encourage you to allow your mind to wonder for ten minutes. Just think of what it would be like literally being in the presence of God. The fact is that no matter how deep, how beautiful, how vast, how glorious the imagination, it still doesn't even come close to who God really is in all of His Glory. Your imagination hasn't even scratched the surface. No wonder why human reasoning can't fathom the splendor of our God. We use less than

10% of our brain and to think that the less than 10% we use can even come close to comprehending the majesty and glory of the God who created the universe, is totally insane! Still, our God who is indescribable allows us to get closer to Him in prayer and He talks to us and guides us into the way that He wants to use us for His glory. What a wonderful God we serve!

I have struggled with the problem of always needing to know and having proof of something before I jumped into it. I was the type of person that if I couldn't make sense of something, I wasn't going to do it period. If a+b did not equal c, it was not for me. There had to be a formula. There was no room for faith in my life what-so-ever. I just had to know everything step by step. I cannot begin to

Chapter 8: "Taking the First Step"

count how many things I had planned out step by step and I've literally missed every step. Everything that I planned out went wrong. Everything I planned fell through. No matter how much my plans didn't work I kept on planning regardless not realizing that my 0 out of 50 record of successful attempts showed that my planning wasn't effective. For some reason, I believed that the more I planned, the more I could predict the outcome, but on the contrary my outcome often times looked nothing like I had planned it to be. I allowed my false expectations to be my hope, instead of placing my hope in Jesus. I tricked myself into believing that if I planned for my future I would know the outcome.

Ta'Sean McKinley

It was not until I gave my will and my ways to God that He not only revealed to me the unknown, but now I know exactly His will is for my life. I don't always know all of the steps that He will take me on, but I do know that the more I seek God for counsel and wisdom, He will reveal what it is that He wants me to do step by step. If only you could see how God is faithful and just to give you an expected end when you are obedient to Him. When God gives you a promise you can expect it to happen. The problem we have with the unknown is that not only is it unpredictable, not only is it unseen, our problem is taking the first step. You have to take the first step and give your life and your will to God and allow Him to lead you. You have to trust

Chapter 8: "Taking the First Step"

God without limits and allow Him to open your eyes and give you the wisdom to follow His will for your life.

What if you could see the plan that God has for your life laid out in front of you? What if God showed you step by step exactly what He was going to do in your life? Then would it be easier to trust Him because all of the answers are right in your face? Of course! You see the process, you know what to expect and you can see the end result of the beauty of what God has for you. This would be ideal but there is one problem with this scenario. There is no room for faith.

We know that without faith it is impossible to please God. (Hebrews 11:6) When we desire to have a road map of God's Journey for us laid out in front of us we are trying to neglect the privilege of having faith. We ultimately are turning down the opportunity to please God by trusting Him and giving up our selfish will and saying yes to His will. Our desire should always be to please God in everything that we do. We should seek to give Him Glory at all times and not seek the approval of men and seeking to please them. We should be so submissive and so God conscious that we don't want to make a move until he tells us to. The Word tells us that we walk by faith and not by sight. Which in its proper context tells us that we can't do both at the same time. You cannot walk by faith if you see where it is your are going at all times. How will you choose to walk?

Chapter 9: "Lacking Prayer"

"And being in an agony he prayed more earnestly: and his sweat was as it were great drops of blood falling down to the ground. And when he rose up from prayer, and was come to his disciples, he found them sleeping for sorrow, And said unto them, Why sleep ye? rise and pray, lest ye enter into temptation."

(Luke 22:44-46 KJV)

Chapter 9: "Lacking Prayer"

Have you ever felt like life was just beating you down? Have you ever had that feeling that you don't know how you are going to get out of the situation that you are currently in? Like you were all alone and your problems had you in a corner just beating you relentlessly. We have all had this experience in life. Either you are going into a situation, going through a situation, or coming out of a situation. I'm sure that one of these categories fits your current position; It's just how life works.

We often neglect prayer when things in our life occur. We get thrown off by the issues of life. Sometimes life packs a huge punch, but it doesn't matter how hard life hits you, what matters is how many hits you can take and keep on fighting. The difference between someone who has reached their purpose and someone that has given up is not that one has an easier fight then the other. It's that the person that reached their purpose never gave up. We all get hit pretty hard sometimes, but it's just one of God's ways to see where our heart is. When things come your way they are not to break you down, but they are to build you up. When a person lifts weights to gain muscle, the muscles first break down and tear in order to heal and build stronger and bigger muscle later.

Let's consider Matthew 14:19 (KJV), "And he commanded the multitude to sit down on the grass, and took the five loaves, and the two fishes, and looking up to heaven, he blessed, brake, and gave the loaves to his disciples, and the disciples to the multitude." The problem

Chapter 9: "Lacking Prayer"

with many of us is that we want to be blessed but we don't want to be broken. We often don't realize that you can't have one without the other.

I remember when I was in high school I didn't have a legit relationship with Christ. I knew of Him but I had never whole heartedly giving my life to Him. When I used to pray I used to try to make deals with God. I would only pray when I felt as though I needed Him to do something urgent for me. I would ultimately try to make bargains like, "God if you help me I won't curse anymore." "God if you get me out of this I won't steal again." These are just simple examples but I used to always try to trade-in a highly desired sin to God. A sin in exchange for help.

Ta'Sean McKinley

Even within my own immaturity and ignorance, I still had a fear of God. I felt that if I had broken my promises he would punish me. Until this day, I can still remember every prayer deal I made with God. That shows how much I didn't pray. It was only three times that I tried to make a deal with God over some foolishness that I got myself into. I remember I went years without praying. I didn't even say my grace before eating my food. For some reason I was so consumed with the world that anything that had to do with God was second to me, so I put in much less effort. God really wasn't even an option in my life. I thought I had everything under control. I felt as though every decision I made was a good decision and that God approved of it.

Chapter 9: "Lacking Prayer"

I came to realize that my life was a mess due to the lack of prayer in my life. Without prayer I was depending on my own intelligence and judgment regarding decisions in my life. This led me down a dark path that was never meant for me. I thank God that his mercy covered me when I was deep in sin, because if it wasn't for his mercy **my ignorance would** have killed me.

It is prayer that keeps us in constant communication with our Father. When we humble ourselves and pray to God, He hears our prayers and He will answer us. God will be faithful to us in instructing us on what it is that He wants us to do. When we pray we yield our hearts to God and allow Him to lead us. It is a guarantee that God will never lead you down the wrong path. So why not follow Him? Why not trust Him? Prayer is one of the best benefits that we have as believers. Prayer allows us to have one-on-one time with The Creator of the heavens and the earth. The Alpha and Omega, The Beginning and The End, The King of kings and The Lord of lords. He who was and is and is to come. Our Lord Jesus Christ.

This one-on-one time with Jesus is where we get to be intimate with Him. This is where we get to spend alone time with Him and get instructions to see what it is that He requires of us. We should count our time of prayer as an honor and a privilege. We shouldn't see prayer as a burden or a waste of time. Prayer is the key for walking in the purpose and destiny that God has for you. Without prayer

Chapter 9: "Lacking Prayer"

there is no way you can be properly instructed to go down the path that God intends for you to walk. When we pray we have the opportunity to know the heart of God. We have that access only through prayer and seeking His will for our lives. Prayer places us in our proper position. When you are praying you are allowing your spirit to line up with the will of God. It is only when you are in line with the will of God that you are in your proper position. Anything outside of the will of God places you on dangerous territory.

It is through prayer and worship that we are able to get away from the cares and the problems of the world. Focused prayer and worship take you away from everything that has you down, because it is in that moment of prayer and worship that your focus becomes on the God who is far above your problems and situations. It is in that moment where you realize that your problems are not really problems. Your problem is the opportunity for God to show up in your life and get the glory out of your situation. The quicker you realize this truth the quicker you will realize that your situation doesn't have the upper hand on you. Your situation is subject to the power and sovereignty of our God. There is nothing to big that Jesus cannot handle. Jesus is right there with us ready to lead the way for us to overcome any problem or adversity that we have in our life. Prayer is very important for the believer. It is our lifeline our open communication

Chapter 9: "Lacking Prayer"

with our King! Will you humble yourself and get in your proper position? Pray!

Chapter 10: "What Did I Sign Up For?"

Chapter 10: "What Did I Sign Up For?"

> "For which of you, intending to build a tower, sitteth not down first, and counteth the cost, whether he have sufficient to finish it?"
>
> (Luke 14:28 KJV)

Ta'Sean McKinley

Throughout this book my prayers are that something was said that changed your life and that you grow closer to Christ. The motive behind why we should do anything should be to honor God and give Him the glory. I am not the kind of person to present a false hope. I don't want to leave you thinking that everything is going to be peaches and cream while walking with Christ, because it's not. It does get challenging at times but, we have to be so grounded in Jesus that no matter what comes our way we won't be shaken or detoured. Being a Christian and following Christ isn't by far the easiest task. Our flesh wants to do the things of the flesh. It doesn't by any means want to yield to The Spirit. That's why we have to constantly be in God's presence to get in tune with His

Chapter 10: "What Did I Sign Up For?"

Holy Spirit. It is important that we discipline ourselves so that we don't go off course. We have to constantly have a hunger and thirst that never goes away for God. We should desire a never-ending fire for God in our hearts so that we will never stop yearning for Him. We have to realize that there is such a need for God that our search for the understanding of God's heart becomes not a priority in our life, but the priority of our life. We should make sure that it actually becomes our life.

As you continue on this journey to grow in God, test and trials will definitely come your way. I guarantee you that you will have obstacles come your way. My brother and/or sister you can overcome any obstacle because you have Jesus there walking with you every step of the way.

We have to submit our will to God's will and we follow him wholeheartedly. A lot of things often times will not make any sense at all. Sometimes God will tell you to do something that is totally off-the-wall and you can't make a rational conclusion out of the situation. This is only a testing of your faith. Once you step out on faith and follow the voice of God, He will prove Himself faithful and will walk along with you throughout the journey. Sometimes our flesh will try to rise up and cause us to question the plan of God, but because you have been in constant communication with Him through prayer, you will have a clear understanding of what it is that He is requiring of you to do. By you having a clear understanding it allows you to resist the flesh's desire to take matters into your own

Chapter 10: "What Did I Sign Up For?"

hands and stand firm on God's word and what it is that He has told you to do.

I can attest that most challenges and tests came once I decided to give my life totally to Christ. I have learned that when we are being tested, it is not to break us but it is to see our hearts condition. When we are tested God intends for us to past the test. He intends for us to use all of the resources and knowledge we have learned leading up to the test. When we are tested with sin and immorality God even gives us a cheat sheet. The bible tells us that He provides for us a way of escape. It is our responsibility as believers to stay focused and use the material we've learned to pass the test. No good teacher gives you a test before first helping you to understand how to solve the answers on the test. It is our responsibility to apply what we have learned and use it for the test.

I had to come to the understanding that God was not breaking me to hurt me, but He was breaking me to build me. He was breaking me to bless me. He was breaking me because there was something that he wanted to bring out of me and he had to break me in order to do it. I encourage you not to neglect or despise the process that God is taking you through. God has a well structured plan as to how your life will go. He has a hand-picked list of tests, trials, blessings etc. strategically planed out just for you, so embrace the process that God Himself has arranged for you. Believe it or not God is cheering for you every time you're being tested. God is right there watching

Chapter 10: "What Did I Sign Up For?"

saying, "go, go, go you can do it! You can make it! I know you can do it!"

There is a process that God wants to take you through and it is totally for your benefit. Will it hurt? Yes! Will you feel pain? Yes! Will you feel like giving up at times! Yes! It is possible to have these feelings. Nevertheless, it will all be worth it. Every ounce of pain, every inch of heart ache is a part of God's process to make you a stronger soldier. I remember when I surrender to God and traded my will to follow his will. I actually sincerely wanted to walk in the purpose that God had for my life and I couldn't do that without totally being sold out for Him. Jesus was all that I wanted. I was willing to leave everything to follow Him. Then He told me what everything was. I walked away from both of my jobs. I've left my family behind. I left my position as the youth pastor at the church I was attending. On top of all that, I had to leave my seven week pregnant wife back in Indianapolis while I went to Atlanta as God instructed. You can only imagine what people said about us, but through it all we remain focused. Not to mention when I left to go to Atlanta I didn't have any family there. I didn't have any friends that lived there. I didn't prepare a place to stay. I slept in my car the first night I got there. I just knew I was going to be homeless. Then to put the icing on the cake; when I went to leave to Atlanta, God told me that I wasn't to work a 9-to-5 job, because I was to totally depend on Him. This was what everything meant. One of the toughest times of my life, but this is what I asked for. I

Chapter 10: "What Did I Sign Up For?"

told God, "I surrender all to you. Whatever you want me to say I'll say. Whatever you want me to do, I'll do. Where ever you want me to go, I'll go." No matter how bad the situation seemed, no matter how things looked, I wouldn't have changed it for the world. It's a privilege to get instructions from the Lord and to be able and willing to follow those instructions.

We all have a choice, to either follow God and allow Him to lead us and guide us. Or to follow our flesh and take it upon ourselves to walk in our own path and neglect the counsel of God. My prayer is that you don't take latter route. My prayer is that you yield to the Holy Spirit and allow Him to be your guide. It definitely won't always be easy, and there will definitely be challenges along the way.

Yet, the reward you will receive for following and obeying God is so much greater and shouldn't even be compared to the little petty trials that we go through along the journey to please God. When pleasing God is all you desire then your challenges should be looked upon as your best friend. If your challenges gives God the glory at the end of the day and your goal is to please Him, you are in good company. If your challenges comes from doing what He told you to do, then you're plan to please God is going perfect and you can guarantee it. God has a divine plan for your life already mapped out for you. You just have to trust Him and go when He tells you to go. Turn where He tells you to turn. Yield when He tells you yield. Stop when

Chapter 10: "What Did I Sign Up For?"

He tells you to stop. Then you will be safely at your destination.

www.ingramcontent.com/pod-product-compliance
Lightning Source LLC
LaVergne TN
LVHW021612080426
835510LV00019B/2528